The Essential Keto

Diet Cookbook 2021

An Essential Guide with Delicious

Recipes for Losing Weight and

Increase your Life Energy

Tanya Scofield

Table of Contents

INTRODUCTION 8

    ASIAN CHICKEN WITH FRESH LIME-PEANUT SAUCE 12

    CHICKEN WITH EGGPLANT & TOMATOES.. 14

    ROSEMARY CHICKEN WITH AVOCADO SAUCE 17

    TASTY CHICKEN WITH BRUSSEL SPROUTS... 19

SIDE DISHES... 22

    CHILI CAULIFLOWER MIX 22

    MOZZARELLA BRUSSELS SPROUTS.. 24

    MOZZARELLA BROCCOLI MIX 26

    PARSLEY BACON BRUSSELS SPROUTS 29

    MEDITERRANEAN SIDE SALAD 32

    MOZZARELLA AND ARTICHOKE MIX.. 34

    ROASTED BRUSSELS SPROUTS 36

    ROSEMARY VEGGIE MIX 38

    CITRIC CAULIFLOWER RICE 39

    ZOODLES SIDE DISH 40

    COCONUT CAULIFLOWER MASH 42

    PARMESAN BRUSSELS SPROUTS... 44

    FRIED CAULIFLOWER RICE 46

    CHEESY ASPARAGUS DISH 48

    ROASTED CAULIFLOWER WITH PROSCIUTTO, CAPERS, AND ALMONDS........................... 49

    KETO JALAPENO POPPERS 52

    BARBECUE FAT BALLS.. 54

    BACON-WRAPPED SCALLOPS.. 56

    LOW CARB TORTILLA PORK RIND WRAPS 58

    AVOCADO CHICKEN SALAD 60

    PALEO-ITALIAN CARPACCIO 62

    MEAT-LOVER PIZZA CUPS 64

    BACON ONION BUTTER 66

    CAESAR EGG SALAD LETTUCE WRAPS 68

    BEST KETO POPCORN CHEESE PUFFS 70

    KETO BACON WRAPPED SALMON WITH PESTO... 72

    DELI FAT BOMBS 74

    KETO LOW CARB TORTILLA CHIPS 76

VEGETABLES.. 78

    TOMATO AND BROCCOLI SOUP 78

BOK CHOY STIR FRY WITH FRIED BACON SLICES 80

BROCCOLI-CAULIFLOWER STEW 82

CREAMY AVOCADO SOUP 84

BOK CHOY MUSHROOM SOUP 86

TASTY RADISH SOUP 88

FRIED GARLICY BACON AND BOK CHOY BROTH 90

NUTRITIONAL MUSTARD GREENS AND SPINACH SOUP 92

HASH BROWNS WITH RADISH 95

BAKED RADISHES 97

COLESLAW AVOCADO SALAD 99

SHERRY WATERCRESS BROTH 102

CREAMED CHEDDAR RADISHES 104

MUSTARD EGG AND AVOCADO SALAD 107

CUCUMBER AVOCADO SALAD MIX 109

FRIED EGGS WITH KALE AND BACON 111

EGGS WITH GREENS 113

SPICY CHAFFLE WITH JALAPENO 115

CONCLUSION 117

The information in the following pages is broadly considered a truthful and accurate account of facts and as such, any inattention, use, or misuse of the information in question by the reader will render any resulting actions solely under their purview. There are no scenarios in which the publisher or the original author of this work can be in any fashion deemed liable for any hardship or damages that may befall them after undertaking information described herein.

Additionally, the information in the following pages is intended only for informational purposes and should thus be thought of as universal. As befitting its nature, it is presented without assurance regarding its prolonged validity or interim quality. Trademarks that are mentioned are done without written consent and can in no way be considered an endorsement from the trademark holder.

INTRODUCTION

So the Ketogenic Diet is all about reducing the amount of carbohydrates you eat. Does this mean you won't get the kind of energy you need for the day? Of course not! It only means that now, your body has to find other possible sources of energy. Do you know where they will be getting that energy? Even before we talk about how to do keto – it's important to first consider why this particular diet works. What actually happens to your body to make you lose weight? As you probably know, the body uses food as an energy source. Everything you eat is turned into energy, so that you can get up and do whatever you need to accomplish for the day. The main energy source is sugar so what happens is that you eat something, the body breaks it down into sugar, and the sugar is processed into energy. Typically, the "sugar" is taken directly from the food you eat so if you eat just the right amount of food, then your body is fueled for the whole day. If you eat too much, then the sugar is stored in your body – hence the accumulation of fat.

But what happens if you eat less food? This is where the Ketogenic Diet comes in. You see, the process of creating sugar from food is usually faster if the food happens to be rich in carbohydrates. Bread, rice, grain, pasta – all of these are carbohydrates and they're the easiest food types to turn into energy.

So here's the situation – you are eating less carbohydrates every day. To keep you energetic, the body breaks down the stored fat and turns them into molecules called ketone bodies. The process of turning the fat into ketone bodies is called "Ketosis" and obviously – this is where the name of the Ketogenic Diet comes from. The ketone bodies take the place of glucose in keeping you energetic. As long as you keep your carbohydrates reduced, the body will keep getting its energy from your body fat.

The Ketogenic Diet is often praised for its simplicity and when you look at it properly, the process is really straightforward. The Science behind the effectivity of the diet is also well-documented, and has been proven multiple times by different medical fields. For example, an article on Diet Review by Harvard provided a lengthy discussion on how the Ketogenic Diet works and why it is so effective for those who choose to use this diet.

But Fat Is the Enemy...Or Is It?

No – fat is NOT the enemy. Unfortunately, years of bad science told us that fat is something you have to avoid – but it's actually a very helpful thing for weight loss! Even before we move forward with this book, we'll have to discuss exactly what "healthy fats" are, and why they're actually the good guys. To do this, we need to make a distinction between the different kinds of fat. You've probably heard of them before and it is a little bit confusing at first. We'll try to go through them as simply as possible:

Saturated fat. This is the kind you want to avoid. They're also called "solid fat" because each molecule is packed with hydrogen atoms. Simply put, it's the kind of fat that can easily cause a blockage in your body. It can raise cholesterol levels and lead to heart problems or a stroke. Saturated fat is something you can find in meat, dairy products, and other processed food items. Now, you're probably wondering: isn't the Ketogenic Diet packed with saturated fat? The answer is: not necessarily. You'll find later in the recipes given that the Ketogenic Diet promotes primarily unsaturated fat or healthy fat. While there are definitely many meat recipes in the list, most of these recipes contain healthy fat sources.

Unsaturated Fat. These are the ones dubbed as healthy fat. They're the kind of fat you find in avocado, nuts, and other ingredients you usually find in Keto-friendly recipes. They're known to lower blood cholesterol and actually come in two types: polyunsaturated and monounsaturated. Both are good for your body but the benefits slightly vary, depending on what you're consuming.

Asian Chicken with Fresh Lime-Peanut Sauce

Preparation Time: 1 HOUR AND 30 MINUTES

Cooking Time: 40 MINUTES

Servings: 6

Ingredients

- 1 tbsp. wheat-free soy sauce
- 1 tbsp. sugar-free fish sauce
- 1 tbsp. lime juice
- 1 tsp coriander
- 1 tsp garlic, minced
- 1 tsp ginger, minced
- 1 tbsp. olive oil
- 1 tbsp. rice wine vinegar
- 1 tsp cayenne pepper
- 1 tbsp. erythritol
- 6 chicken thighs
- **Sauce:**
- ½ cup peanut butter
- 1 tsp garlic, minced
- 1 tbsp. lime juice

- 2 tbsp. water
- 1 tsp ginger, minced
- 1 tbsp. jalapeño, chopped
- 2 tbsp. rice wine vinegar
- 2 tbsp. erythritol
- 1 tbsp. fish sauce

Directions

1. Combine all of the chicken ingredients in a large Ziploc bag.
2. Seal the bag and shake to combine.
3. Refrigerate for about 1 hour.
4. Remove from the fridge about 15 minutes before cooking.
5. Preheat the grill to medium, and grill the chicken for about 7 minutes per side.
6. Meanwhile, whisk together all of the sauce ingredients in a mixing bowl.
7. Serve the chicken drizzled with peanut sauce.

Nutrition Calories 492, Net Carbs 3g, Fat 36g, Protein 35g

Chicken with Eggplant & Tomatoes

Preparation Time: 25 MINUTES

Cooking Time: 10 MINUTES

Servings: 4

Ingredients

- 2 tbsp. ghee
- 1 lb. chicken thighs
- Salt and black pepper to taste
- 2 cloves garlic, minced
- 1 (14 oz.) can whole tomatoes
- 1 eggplant, diced
- 10 fresh basil leaves, chopped + extra to garnish

Directions

1. Melt ghee in a saucepan over medium heat, season the chicken with salt and black pepper, and fry for 4 minutes on each side until golden brown. Remove the chicken onto a plate.
2. Sauté the garlic in the ghee for 2 minutes, pour in the tomatoes, and cook covered for 8 minutes.

Include the eggplant and basil. Cook for 4 minutes.

3. Season the sauce with salt and black pepper, stir and add the chicken. Coat with sauce and simmer for 3 minutes.

4. Serve chicken with sauce on a bed of squash pasta garnished with basil.

Nutrition Calories 468, Net Carbs 2g, Fat 39.5g, Protein 26g

Rosemary Chicken with Avocado Sauce

Preparation Time: 22 MINUTES

Cooking Time: 30 MINUTES

Servings: 4 |

Ingredients

- 1 avocado pitted
- ½ cup mayonnaise
- 3 tbsp. ghee
- 4 chicken breasts
- Salt and black pepper to taste
- 1 cup rosemary, chopped
- ½ cup chicken broth

Directions

1. Spoon avocado, mayonnaise, and salt into a food processor and puree until a smooth sauce is derived. Adjust the taste with salt. Pour sauce into a jar and refrigerate.
2. Melt ghee in a large skillet, season chicken with salt and black pepper, and fry for 4 minutes on

each side to a golden brown. Remove chicken to a plate.

3. Pour the broth in the same skillet and add the cilantro. Bring to simmer covered for 3 minutes and add the chicken. Cover, and cook on low heat for 5 minutes until the liquid has reduced and chicken is fragrant.

4. Dish chicken only into serving plates and spoon the mayo-avocado sauce over.

5. Serve warm with buttered green beans and baby carrots.

Nutrition Calories 398, Net Carbs 4g, Fat 32g, Protein 24g

Tasty Chicken with Brussel Sprouts

Preparation Time: 120 MINUTES

Cooking Time: 40 MINUTES

Servings: 8

Ingredients

- 5 pounds whole chicken
- 1 bunch oregano
- 1 bunch thyme
- 1 tbsp. marjoram
- 1 tbsp. parsley
- 1 tbsp. olive oil
- 2 pounds Brussel sprouts
- 1 lemon
- 4 tbsp. butter

Directions

1. Preheat your oven to 450 F.
2. Stuff the chicken with oregano, thyme, and lemon.
3. Make sure the wings are tucked over and behind.

---

4. Roast for 15 minutes. Reduce the heat to 325 F, and cook for 40 minutes.

5. Spread the butter over the chicken and sprinkle parsley and marjoram.

6. Add the Brussel sprouts. Return to oven and bake for 40 more minutes.

7. Let sit for 10 minutes before carving.

Nutrition Calories 430, Net Carbs 5g, Fat 32g, Protein 30g

SIDE DISHES

Chili Cauliflower Mix

Preparation Time: 10 minutes

Cooking Time: 35 minutes

Servings: 4

Ingredients:

- 2 tablespoons sweet chili sauce
- 3 tablespoons olive oil
- 3 garlic cloves, minced
- Juice of 1 lime
- 1 cauliflower head, florets separated
- 1 teaspoon cilantro, chopped
- A pinch of salt and black pepper

Directions:

1. In a bowl, the chili sauce with the oil, garlic, lime juice, salt, pepper, cilantro and the cauliflower, toss well, spread on a lined baking sheet, introduce in the oven and cook at 425 degrees F for 35 minutes.

2. Divide the cauliflower between plates and serve as a side dish.

Nutrition: Calories: 271 Fat: 4 Fiber: 7, Carbohydrates: 11 Protein: 7

Mozzarella Brussels Sprouts

Preparation Time: 10 minutes

Cooking Time: 30 minutes

Servings: 6

Ingredients:

- 2 tablespoons olive oil
- 2 pounds Brussels sprouts
- 2 garlic cloves, minced
- 1 teaspoon thyme, chopped
- A pinch of salt and black pepper
- 1 cup mozzarella, shredded
- ¼ cup parmesan, grated
- 1 tablespoon parsley, chopped

Directions:

1. Put some water in a pot, bring to a boil over medium-high heat, add sprouts, cook them for 10 minutes, transfer them to a bowl filled with ice water, cool them down and drain them well.

2. In a bowl, combine the Brussels sprouts with salt, pepper, oil, garlic and thyme, toss and smash them a bit.

3. Spread smashed Brussels sprouts on a lined baking sheet, sprinkle mozzarella and parmesan on top, introduce in the oven and bake them at 425 degrees F for 20 minutes.

4. Sprinkle parsley on top, divide between plates and serve as a side dish.

Nutrition: Calories: 288 Fat: 4 Fiber: 6 Carbohydrates: 13Protein: 6

Mozzarella Broccoli Mix

Preparation Time: 10 minutes

Cooking Time: 15 minutes

Servings: 4

Ingredients:

- 2 tablespoons olive oil
- 1 broccoli head, florets separated
- 2 garlic cloves, minced
- ½ cup mozzarella, shredded
- ¼ cup parmesan, grated
- ½ cup coconut cream
- 1 tablespoon parsley, chopped

Directions:

1. Heat up a pan with the oil over medium-high heat add broccoli, salt, pepper and garlic, stir and cook for 6 minutes.
2. Add parmesan, mozzarella and cream, toss, introduce the pan in the oven and cook at 375 degrees F for 10 minutes.
3. Add parsley, toss, divide between plates and serve as a side dish.

Nutrition: Calories: 261 Fat: 4 Fiber: 4
Carbohydrates: 13 Protein: 8

Parsley Bacon Brussels Sprouts

Preparation Time: 10 minutes

Cooking Time: 20 minutes

Servings: 6

Ingredients:

- 1-pound Brussels sprouts, halved
- A pinch of salt and black pepper
- 7 bacon slices, chopped
- 1 yellow onion, chopped
- 2 tablespoons stevia
- 2 tablespoons olive oil
- 1 tablespoon parsley, chopped
- 2 teaspoons sweet paprika

Directions:

1. Heat up a pan with the oil over medium-high heat, add the onion, stir and sauté for 4-5 minutes.
2. Add the bacon, stir and cook for 3 minutes more.
3. Add the sprouts, salt, pepper, stevia, paprika and parsley, toss, cook for 10 minutes more, divide between plates and serve as a side dish.

Nutrition: Calories: 261   Fat: 4   Fiber: 8
Carbohydrates: 12 Protein: 8

Mediterranean Side Salad

Preparation Time: 10 minutes

Cooking Time: 0 minutes

Servings: 4

Ingredients:

- 1-pint cherry tomatoes, halved
- 1 cup kalamata olives, pitted and sliced
- 1 cucumber, sliced
- ½ red onion, sliced
- 1 cup feta cheese, crumbled
- Juice of ½ lemon
- 2 tablespoons red vinegar
- A pinch of salt and black pepper
- 1 teaspoon oregano, dried
- ¼ cup olive oil

Directions:

1. In a salad bowl, combine the tomatoes with the olives, cucumber and onion.
2. In a separate bowl, combine the lemon juice with the vinegar, salt, pepper, oregano and oil and whisk well.

3. Pour this over your salad, toss, sprinkle cheese at the end and serve as a side dish.

Nutrition: Calories: 200 Fat: 3 Fiber: 6 Carbohydrates: 12 Protein: 8

Mozzarella and Artichoke Mix

Preparation Time: 10 minutes

Cooking Time: 10 minutes

Servings: 4

Ingredients:

- 14 ounces canned artichoke hearts, drained
- A pinch of salt and black pepper
- 2 cups baby spinach
- 2 tablespoons parsley, chopped
- 1 cup mozzarella, shredded
- Juice of 1 lemon
- 1 and ¾ cup coconut milk
- ½ cup chicken stock
- 2 garlic cloves, minced
- 3 tablespoons ghee, melted
- A pinch of red pepper flakes

Directions:

1. Heat up a pan with the ghee over medium-high heat, add the garlic, stir and cook for 2 minutes.
2. Add lemon juice, coconut milk, stock, artichokes, salt and pepper, stir and cook for 5 minutes.

3. Add spinach, pepper flakes and mozzarella, toss, cook for 3 minutes more, and divide between plates, sprinkle parsley on top and serve as a side dish.

Nutrition: Calories: 277 Fat: 3 Fiber: 6 Carbohydrates: 12 Protein: 8

Roasted Brussels Sprouts

Preparation Time: 10 minutes

Cooking Time: 25 minutes

Servings: 4

Ingredients:

- 1-pound Brussels sprouts, halved
- 2 tablespoons olive oil
- A pinch of salt and black pepper

Directions:

1. Spread the sprouts on a lined baking sheet, add the oil, salt and pepper, toss, introduce in the oven and bake at 425 degrees F for 25 minutes.
2. Divide between plates and serve as a side dish.

Nutrition: Calories: 200 Fat: 2 Fiber: 6 Carbohydrates: 11 Protein: 8

Rosemary Veggie Mix

Preparation Time: 10 minutes

Cooking Time: 20 minutes

Servings: 4

Ingredients:

- 1-pound Brussels sprouts, halved
- 2 tablespoons olive oil
- 1 teaspoon rosemary, chopped
- 1 tablespoon balsamic vinegar
- 1 teaspoon thyme, chopped
- ½ cup cranberries, dried

Directions:

1. Spread the sprouts on a lined baking sheet, add rosemary, vinegar, oil and thyme, toss, introduce in the oven and cook at 400 degrees F for 20 minutes.
2. Divide between plates, sprinkle cranberries on top and serve as a side dish.

Nutrition: Calories: 199 Fat: 3 Fiber: 5 Carbohydrates: 12 Protein: 7

Citric Cauliflower Rice

Preparation Time: 10 minutes

Cooking Time: 15 minutes

Servings: 4

Ingredients:

- 1 tablespoon ghee, melted
- Juice of 2 limes
- A pinch of salt and black pepper
- 1 cup cauliflower rice
- 1 and ½ cups veggie stock
- 1 tablespoon cilantro, chopped

Directions:

1. Heat up a pan with the ghee over medium-high heat, add the cauliflower rice, stir and cook for 5 minutes.
2. Add lime juice, salt, pepper and stock, stir, bring to a simmer and cook for 10 minutes.
3. Add cilantro, toss, divide between plates and serve as a side dish.

Nutrition: Calories: 200 Fat: 3 Fiber: 6 Carbohydrates: 9 Protein: 6

Zoodles Side Dish

Preparation Time: 10 minutes

Cooking Time: 0 minutes

Servings: 4

Ingredients:

- 4 zucchinis, cut with a spiralizer
- 2 tablespoons olive oil
- A pinch of salt and black pepper
- 1 cup mozzarella, shredded
- 2 cups cherry tomatoes, halved
- ¼ cup basil, torn
- 2 tablespoons balsamic vinegar

Directions:

1. In a bowl, combine the zucchini noodles with salt, pepper and the oil, toss and leave aside for 10 minutes.

2. Add mozzarella, tomatoes, basil and vinegar, toss, divide between plates and serve as a side dish.

Nutrition: Calories: 188 Fat: 6 Fiber: 8 Carbohydrates: 8 Protein: 6

Coconut Cauliflower Mash

Preparation Time: 10 minutes

Cooking Time: 10 minutes

Servings: 6

Ingredients:

- 2 cauliflower heads, florets separated
- 1/3 cup coconut cream
- 1/3 cup coconut milk
- 1 tablespoon chives, chopped
- A pinch of salt and black pepper

Directions:

1. Put some water in a pot, bring to a boil over medium-high heat, add cauliflower florets, cook them for 10 minutes, drain them well, mash using a potato masher and stir.
2. Add the cream, the coconut milk, salt, pepper and chives, stir well, divide between plates and serve as a side dish.

Nutrition: Calories: 200 Fat: 3 Fiber: 3 Carbohydrates: 12 Protein: 5

Parmesan Brussels Sprouts

Preparation Time: 10 minutes

Cooking Time: 30 minutes

Servings: 4

Ingredients:

- 1-pound Brussels sprouts, halved
- 1 teaspoon oregano, dried
- 1 tablespoon olive oil
- 3 garlic cloves, minced
- ½ teaspoon hot paprika
- A pinch of salt and black pepper
- 2 tablespoons keto ranch dressing
- 1 tablespoon parmesan, grated

Directions:

1. Spread the sprouts on a lined baking sheet, add oregano, oil, garlic, paprika, salt and pepper, toss, bake them in the oven at 425 degrees F for 30 minutes, add parmesan and keto ranch dressing, toss well, divide between plates and serve as a side dish.

Nutrition: Calories: 222 Fat: 4 Fiber: 6 Carbohydrates: 12 Protein: 8

Fried Cauliflower Rice

Preparation Time: 10 minutes

Cooking Time: 15 minutes

Servings: 4

Ingredients:

- 1 tablespoon ghee, melted
- 1 small yellow onion, chopped
- 2 hot dogs, sliced
- 1 tablespoon avocado oil
- 1 garlic clove, minced
- 2 and ½ cups cauliflower rice, steamed
- 2 eggs, whisked
- 2 tablespoons coconut amino
- 2 scallions, sliced

Directions:

1. Heat up a pan with the ghee over medium-high heat, add onion, garlic and hot dogs, stir and cook for 5 minutes.
2. Add cauliflower rice and avocado oil, stir and cook for 5 minutes more.

3. Add the eggs, toss everything, and cook for 5 more minutes until the eggs are scrambled, add the amino and the scallions, toss, divide between plates and serve as a side dish.

Nutrition: Calories: 200 Fat: 3 Fiber: 6 Carbohydrates: 12 Protein: 8

Cheesy Asparagus Dish

Preparation Time: 10 minutes

Cooking Time: 30 minutes

Servings: 6

Ingredients:

- 3 garlic cloves, minced
- ¾ cup coconut cream
- 2 pounds asparagus, trimmed
- 1 cup parmesan, grated
- A pinch of salt and black pepper
- 1 cup mozzarella, shredded

Directions:

1. In a baking dish, combine the asparagus with the garlic, cream, salt, pepper, mozzarella and top with the parmesan, introduce in the oven and bake at 400 degrees F for 30 minutes.
2. Divide between plates and serve as a side dish.

Nutrition: Calories: 200 Fat: 3 Fiber: 6 Carbohydrates: 12 Protein: 9

Roasted Cauliflower with Prosciutto, Capers, and Almonds.

Preparation Time: 10 minutes

Cooking Time: 25 minutes

Servings: 2

Ingredients:

- 12 ounces cauliflower florets (I get precut florets at Trader Joe's)
- 2 tablespoons leftover bacon grease, or olive oil
- Pink Himalayan salt
- Freshly ground black pepper
- 2 ounces sliced prosciutto, torn into small pieces
- ¼ cup slivered almonds
- 2 tablespoons capers
- 2 tablespoons grated Parmesan cheese

Directions:

1. Preheat the oven to 400 degrees F. Line a baking pan with a silicone baking mat or parchment paper.
2. Put the cauliflower florets in the prepared baking pan with the bacon grease, and season with pink

---

Himalayan salt and pepper. Or if you are using olive oil instead, drizzle the cauliflower with olive oil and season with pink Himalayan salt and pepper.

3. Roast the cauliflower for 15 minutes.

4. Stir the cauliflower so all sides are coated with the bacon grease.

5. Distribute the prosciutto pieces in the pan. Then add the slivered almonds and capers. Stir to combine. Sprinkle the Parmesan cheese on top, and roast for 10 minutes more.

6. Divide between two plates, using a slotted spoon so you don't get excess grease in the plates, and serve.

Nutrition: Calories: 288 Fat: 24g Carbohydrates: 7 Fiber: 3 Protein: 14

Keto Jalapeno Poppers

Preparation Time: 10 minutes

Cooking Time: 20 minutes

Serving: 16

Ingredients

- 8 oz. cream cheese
- 1/2 cup shredded sharp cheddar cheese
- 1 tsp pink himalayan salt
- 1/2 tsp black pepper
- 8 jalapenos, halved, de-seeded
- 8 slices of bacon, cut in half

Directions:

1. Preheat stove to 375 degrees and line heating sheet with material paper.

2. Spot bacon cuts on paper towel-lined plate and microwave for 3 minutes. Put aside to somewhat cool.

3. In a medium bowl, include cream cheddar, destroyed sharp cheddar, salt, and pepper and microwave for 15 seconds. Mix together

4. Cautiously scoop cream cheddar blend into a plastic baggie

5. Wrap bacon cuts around jalapenos and stick with a toothpick.

6. Spot jalapenos on arranged heating sheet and prepare for 15 minutes.

7. Increment broiler warmth to cook and sear for 2-3 minutes, watching to guarantee cream cheddar doesn't consume.

8. Remove from broiler and permit cooling marginally before eating.

Nutrition Calories 79 Fat 6.6g, Carbs 2.1g, Protein 8g

Barbecue Fat Balls

Preparation Time: 5 minutes

Cooking Time: 0 minutes

Serving: 6

Ingredients

- 4 ounces cream cheese
- 4 tbsp. bacon fat
- ½ tsp smoke flavor
- 2 drops stevia
- 1/8 tsp apple cider vinegar
- 1 tbsp. sweet smoked chili powder

Directions:

1. In a food processor, process all ingredients except chili powder until they form a smooth cream.
2. Scrap mixture and transfer into a small bowl, then refrigerate for 2 hours.
3. Form into 6 balls.
4. Sprinkle balls with chili powder, roll to coat well.
5. Serve.

Nutrition Calories 146 Fat 14g Carbs 1.5g Protein 1.3g

Bacon-Wrapped Scallops

Preparation Time: 10 minutes

Cooking Time: 15 minute

Serving: 4

Ingredients

- 16 sea scallops
- 8 slices bacon
- 16 toothpicks
- olive oil for drizzling
- black pepper and kosher salt to taste

Directions:

1. Preheat broiler to 425°F.

2. Line a heating sheet with material paper. Put in a safe spot.

3. Envelop one scallop by using a half-reduce of bacon and comfortable with a toothpick.

4. Shower olive oil over every scallop and season with pepper and valid salt.

5. Orchestrate scallops in a solitary layer on a readied preparing sheet, giving every scallop some space to permit the bacon to clean.

6. Heat 12 to 15mins until scallop is sensitive and bacon is cooked through. Serve hot.

Nutrition Calories 224 Fat 17g, Carbs 2g, Protein 12g

Low Carb Tortilla Pork Rind Wraps

Preparation Time: 10 minutes

Cooking Time: 30 minutes

Serving: 8 wraps

Ingredients

- 4 large eggs
- 3 ounces pork rinds
- ½ tsp garlic powder
- ¼ tsp ground cumin
- ¼ to ½ cup water

- avocado oil or coconut oil

Directions:

1. In a powerful blender or nourishment processor, consolidate the eggs, pork skins, garlic powder, and cumin. Mix until smooth and very much joined. Include 1/4 cup of the water and mix once more. On the off chance that the blend is extremely thick, keep on including water until it is the consistency of hotcake hitter.

2. Warmth a sparse 1/2 teaspoon of oil in an 8-inch nonstick skillet over medium-low warmth, include around 3 tablespoons of the hitter and utilize an elastic spatula to spread it meagerly over the base of the dish, nearly to the edges.

3. Cook for about a moment, until the base is starting to dark-colored.

4. Rehash with the rest of the player, adding oil to the skillet just as essential

5. Add more water to the player as required; it will thicken as it sits.

Nutrition Calories 194, Fat 5.6g, Carbs 5.4g, Protein 9.7g

Avocado Chicken Salad

Preparation Time: 15 minutes

Cooking Time: 20 minutes

Serving: 3

Ingredients

- 3 avocados
- 1 lb. chicken (cooked in any way from this book)
- 1 medium tomato
- 1 onion
- 4 limes
- sea salt and fresh ground black pepper

Directions:

1. In an enormous bowl pound the avocados until smooth.

2. Include the chicken, onions, tomatoes, lime squeeze, salt, and pepper.

3. Blend well.

Nutrition Calories 465, Fat 38g, Carbs 6.7g, Protein 55g

Paleo-Italian Carpaccio

Preparation Time: 1hour 30 minutes

Cooking Time: 1 hour

Serving: 4

Ingredients

- 8 ounces of grass-fed, grass-finished filet mignon

- 1 bunch fresh organic Arugula

- 4 tsp truffle infused extra virgin olive oil

- 1 tsp unrefined sea salt

- freshly ground black pepper to taste

Directions:

1. Spot the meat in the cooler for around 2 hours. This will make it firm enough to cut with a sharp gourmet specialist's blade or with a meat slicer.
2. Cut meagerly and isolate the individual cuts laying them on 4 individual plates.
3. Organize the arugula over the meat, separating it similarly
4. Shower the oil on the plates, at that point sprinkle with salt and pepper
5. In the event that you are utilizing cheddar, mastermind the shaved parmesan on top
6. You can include extra naturally ground dark pepper to decorate the top.
7. Plates can be chilled in the icebox for 30 minutes before serving.

Nutrition Calories 437, Fat 28g, Carbs 4g, Protein 31g

Meat-Lover Pizza Cups

Preparation Time: 15 minutes

Cooking Time: 11 minutes

Serving: 12

Ingredients

- 12 deli ham slices
- 1 lb. bulk Italian sausages
- 12 tbsp. sugar-free pizza sauce
- 3 cups grated mozzarella cheese
- 24 pepperoni slices

- 1 cup cooked and crumbled bacon

Directions:

1. Preheat broiler to 375 F. Fry Italian frankfurters in a skillet, depleting abundance oil.

2. Line 12-cup biscuit tin with ham cuts. Italian sausages, ham slices, pizza sauce, mozzarella cheese, pepperoni cuts, and bacon disintegrate between each cup, in a specific order.

3. Heat at 375 F for 10 minutes, cook for 1 moment until cheese air pockets and tans and the edges of the meat ingredients look firm.

4. Remove pizza cups from biscuit tin and set on paper towels to keep the bottoms from getting wet.

5. Serve.

Nutrition Calories 165, Fat 14g, Carbs 6.1g, Protein 2g

Bacon Onion Butter

Preparation Time: 15 minutes

Cooking Time: 35 minutes

Serving: 6

Ingredients

- 9 tbsp. butter
- 4 strips bacon sliced into small strips
- 90 grams onion
- 2 tsp spicy brown mustard
- 1/2 tsp black pepper

Directions:

1. Dissolve 1 tablespoon margarine in a skillet on medium warmth and include bacon pieces.

2. When the bacon fat is beginning to cook include diced onion and fry until onion and bacon are fresh yet not overcooked.

3. Put aside bacon/onion blend in a bowl and cool to room temp.

4. Include mellowed margarine, 8 tablespoons, to an enormous blending bowl.

5. Include bacon and onions, yellow mustard, and pepper.

6. Cream together ingredients or utilize an electric blender.

7. Spoon into a smaller than normal biscuit tin, place in cooler until margarine is strong again.

Nutrition Calories 830, Fat 117g, Carbs 7.0g, Protein 15g

Caesar Egg Salad Lettuce Wraps

Preparation Time: 10 minutes

Cooking Time: 15 minutes

Serving: 4

Ingredients

- 6 large hard-boiled eggs
- 3 tbsp. creamy Caesar dressing
- 3 tbsp. mayonnaise
- 1/2 cup Parmesan cheese
- cracked black pepper
- 4 large romaine lettuce leaves

Directions:

1. In a blending bowl, join hacked eggs, velvety Caesar dressing, mayonnaise, and 1/4 cup Parmesan cheddar and broke dark pepper.
2. Spoon blend onto romaine leaves and top with residual Parmesan cheddar.

Nutrition Calories 254, Fat 22g, Carbs 2.7g, Protein 13.5g

Best Keto Popcorn Cheese Puffs

Preparation Time: 5 minutes

Cooking Time: 5 minutes

Servings: 4

Ingredients

- 4 ounces cheddar cheese sliced

Directions:

1. Cut the cheddar into little ¼ inch squares.

2. Prior to heating, this formula must be readied 24 hours in advance

3. Cover the pan with baking parchment.

4. Leave the cheddar to dry out for in any event 24 hours.

5. The following day preheat your stove to 200C/390F and heat the cheddar for 3-5 minutes until it is puffed up.

6. Leave to cool for 10 minutes before getting a charge out of.

Nutrition Calories 114, Fat 9g, Carbs 2.2g, Protein 7g

Keto Bacon Wrapped Salmon with Pesto

Preparation Time: 5 minutes

Cooking Time: 15 minutes

Serving: 1

Ingredients

- 170g salmon fillet
- 1 slice streaky bacon
- 2 tbsp. pesto

Directions:

1. Spot the streaky bacon on a hacking board.
2. Spot the salmon filet over the bacon. Move up firmly and comfy with a wooden stick.

3. Spot 1-2 tbsp. pesto inside the center.

4. Spot in the skillet, unfold, and fry tenderly for 10 minutes until the salmon and bacon are cooked. There is not any compelling motive to show the keto bacon-wrapped salmon. At the factor when you prepare dinner it in the griddle with the top, on medium warm temperature, it'll permit the steam internal to cook dinner the salmon from above.

5. Then again, region the bacon-wrapped salmon on a covered making ready plate/sheet container within the stove at 180C/350F for 15mins

Nutrition Calories 449, Fat 31g, Carbs 3g, Protein 38g

Deli Fat Bombs

Preparation Time: 5 minutes

Cooking Time: 0 minutes

Serving: 2

Ingredients

- 8 (1-ounce) slices sugar-free deli ham

- 4 ounces chive cream cheese

- 1 cup chopped baby spinach

- 1 medium red bell pepper, seeded and sliced

Directions:

1. Lay out each slice of ham flat. Spread 1 tbsp. cream cheese on each slice.
2. Put 2 tbsp. chopped spinach on top of the cream cheese on each slice.
3. Divide bell pepper into 8 portions and put the portions on top of spinach.
4. Roll up the ham and secure with a toothpick.
5. Serve.

Nutrition Calories 399, Fat 25.9g, Carbs 6.7g, Protein 23.2g

Keto Low Carb Tortilla Chips

Preparation Time: 10 minutes

Cooking Time: 7 minutes

Servings: 8

Ingredients

- 2 cups mozzarella
- 3/4 cup almond flour
- 1/4 tsp onion, garlic and paprika
- 2 tbsp. psyllium husk Pinch salt

Directions:

1. Warmth you're stove to 350F.
2. Dissolve the mozzarella in the microwave. On the other hand, heat delicately in a non-stick pot.

3. Include the almond flour/ground almonds and psyllium husk in addition to the salt and flavors, if utilizing. Mix until consolidated, at that point ply until you have a smooth mixture.

4. Separate the batter into 2 balls and turn out between 2 sheets of preparing/material paper. Turn out as meagerly as could be expected under the circumstances! The more slender, the crispier your tortilla chips will turn out.

5. Cut into triangles and spread out on a sheet of preparing paper so the tortilla chips don't contact.

6. Prepare 6-8 minutes or until sautéed on the edges. Heating time will rely upon the thickness of your tortilla chips. I heated mine in 2 rounds, in addition to a third-round for the off-cuts.

Nutrition Calories 143, Fat 9.2g, Carbs 4.8g, Protein 8.3g

VEGETABLES

Tomato and broccoli soup

Preparation Time: 50 minutes

Cooking Time: 55 minutes

Servings: 4

Ingredients:

- A drizzle of olive oil
- Canned sugar-free tomatoes- 28 oz.
- Crushed red pepper- ¼ tsp.
- Broccoli head: into florets- 1
- Small ginger: chopped- 1
- Onion: chopped – 1
- Garlic clove: minced- 1
- Coriander seeds- 2 tsp.
- Black pepper
- Salt

Directions:

1. Boil water and salt in a pan on medium-high and add broccoli florets to steam for 2 minutes.

2. Remove and put in a bowl of ice water. Drain and set aside.

3. Heat pan and put in coriander seeds to toast for 4 minutes. Blend in a blender and set aside.

4. Pour olive oil in a pot and set to medium and add red pepper, salt, pepper and onions and cook for 7 minutes.

5. Mix in coriander seeds and garlic and let it cook for 3 minutes.

6. Pour in tomatoes and let simmer for 10 minutes.

7. Mix in broccoli and cook for 12 minutes.

8. Serve

Nutrition: Calories- 152, carbs- 1, protein- 9, fiber- 8, fats- 9

Bok Choy Stir Fry with Fried Bacon Slices

Preparation Time: 17 minutes

Cooking Time: 15 minutes

Servings: 2

Ingredients:

- Bok choy; chopped - 2 cup.
- Garlic cloves; minced - 2
- Bacon slices; chopped - 2
- A drizzle of avocado oil
- Salt and black pepper to the taste.

Instructions:

1. Take a pan and heat it with oil over medium heat.
2. When the oil is hot, add bacon and keep stirring it until it's brown and crispy.
3. Transfer them to paper towels to drain out the excess oil.
4. Now bring the pan to medium heat and in it add garlic and bok choy.
5. Again give it a stir and cook it for 5 minutes.

6. Now drizzle and add some salt, pepper and the fried bacon and stir them for another 1 minute.

7. Turn off the heat and divide them in plates to serve.

Nutrition Calories: 50; Fat: 1; Fiber: 1; Carbs: 2; Protein: 2

Broccoli-cauliflower stew

Preparation Time: 25 minutes

Cooking Time: 15 minutes

Servings: 5

Ingredients:

- Bacon slices: chopped -2
- Cauliflower head: separated into florets- 1
- Broccoli head: separated into florets- 1
- Butter- 2 tbsp.
- Garlic cloves: minced- 2
- Salt
- Black pepper

Directions:

1. Put a pan on medium heat and dissolve the butter and the garlic. Add the bacon slices to brown for 3 minutes all over.
2. Mix in broccoli and cauliflower florets to cook for 2 minutes.
3. Pour water over it and cover the lid and let cook for 10 minutes.

4. Season with pepper and salt and puree soup with a dipping blend.

5. Let boil slowly for some minutes on medium heat.

6. Serve into bowls.

Nutrition: Calories- 128, carbs- 4, protein- 6, fiber- 7, fats- 2

Creamy Avocado Soup

Preparation Time: 20 minutes

Cooking Time: 15 minutes

Servings: 4

Ingredients:

- Chicken stock, 3 c.
- Black pepper
- Chopped scallions, 2
- Salt
- Heavy cream, 2/3 c.
- Butter, 2 tbsps.
- Chopped avocados, 2

Directions:

1. Over a medium source of heat, set the saucepan and cook the scallions for 2 minutes
2. Stir in 2 ½ cups stock to simmer for 3 minutes
3. Set the blender in position to blend avocados, heavy cream, the remaining stock, and seasonings.
4. Return to a pan to cook for 2 minutes as you adjust the seasoning

5. Serve in soup bowls

Nutrition: Calories: 335, Fat: 32, Fiber: 9, Carbs: 13, Protein: 3

Bok choy mushroom soup

Preparation Time: 25 minutes

Cooking Time: 15 minutes

Servings: 4

Ingredients:

- Bacon strips: chopped- 2

- Beef stock- 3 cups

- Bok choy: chopped- 1 bunch

- Onion: chopped- 1

- Parmesan cheese: grated- 3 tbsp.

- Coconut aminos- 3 tbsp.

- Worcestershire sauce- 2 tbsp.

- Red pepper flakes- ½ tbsp.

- Mushrooms: chopped- 1½ cups

- Black Pepper

- Salt

Directions:

1. Put bacon in a saucepan over medium-high heat to brown until crispy then remove to paper towels to drain.

2. To medium heat, add the mushrooms and onions in the pan and cook for 15 minutes.

3. Pour in the stock, pepper flakes, aminos, bok choy, Worcestershire sauce, salt and pepper and mix.

4. Cook until bok choy is tender.

5. Serve into bowls and sprinkle with Parmesan cheese and bacon.

Nutrition: Calories- 100, carbs- 1, protein- 5, fiber- 9, fats- 5

Tasty Radish Soup

Preparation Time: 30 minutes

Cooking Time: 45 minutes

Servings: 4

Ingredients:

- Chopped onion, 1
- Salt
- Chopped celery stalk, 2
- Chicken stock, 6 c.
- Coconut oil, 3 tbsps.
- Quartered radishes, 2 bunches
- Black pepper
- Minced garlic cloves, 6

Directions:

1. Set the pan over medium heat and melt the oil
2. Stir in the celery, onion, and garlic to cook until soft, about 5 minutes
3. Stir in the stock, radishes, and seasonings.
4. Cover and simmer to boil for 15 minutes
5. Enjoy while still hot

Nutrition: Calories: 131, Fat: 12, Fiber: 8, Carbs: 4, Protein: 1

Fried garlicy bacon and bok choy broth

Preparation Time: 17 minutes

Cooking Time: 15 minutes

Servings: 2

Ingredients:

- Bok choy: chopped- 2 cups
- A drizzle of avocado oil
- Bacon slices: chopped- 2
- Garlic cloves: minced- 2
- Black pepper
- Salt

Directions:

1. Put bacon in a pan on medium heat and let crisp. Remove and let drain on paper towels.
2. Add bok choy and garlic to the pan and let cook for 4 minutes.
3. Season with pepper and salt and put the bacon back into the pan.
4. Let cook for 1 minute and serve.

Nutrition: Calories- 116, carbs- 8, protein- 3, fiber- 8, fats- 1

Nutritional Mustard Greens and Spinach Soup

Preparation Time: 25 minutes

Cooking Time: 15 minutes

Servings: 6

Ingredients:

- Spinach; torn - 5 cups.
- Fenugreek seeds - 1/2 teaspoon.
- Cumin seeds - 1 teaspoon.
- Jalapeno; chopped - 1 tablespoon.
- Mustard greens; chopped - 5 cups.
- Ghee - 2 teaspoons.
- Paprika - 1/2 teaspoon.
- Avocado oil - 1 tablespoon.
- Coriander seeds - 1 teaspoon.
- Yellow onion; chopped - 1 cup.
- Garlic; minced - 1 tablespoon.
- Ginger; grated - 1 tablespoon.
- Turmeric; ground - 1/2 teaspoon.
- Coconut milk - 3 cups.
- Salt and black pepper to the taste.

Directions:

1. Add coriander, fenugreek and cumin seed in a heated pot with oil over medium high heat.
2. Now stir and brow them for 2 minutes.
3. In the same pot, add onions and again stir them for 3 minutes.
4. Now after the onion's cooked, add half of the garlic, jalapenos, ginger and turmeric.
5. Again, give it a good stir and cook for another 3 minutes.
6. Add some more mustard greens, spinach and saute everything for 10 minutes.
7. After it's done add milk, salt, pepper before blending the soup with an immersion blender.
8. Now take another pan and heat it up over medium heat with some ghee drizzled on it.
9. In it, add garlic, paprika, and give it a good stir before turning off the heat.
10. Bring the soup to heat over medium heat and transfer them into soup bowls.

11.Top it with some drizzles of ghee and paprika. Now it's ready to serve hot.

Nutrition: Calories: - 143; Fat: 6; Fiber: 3; Carbs: 7; Protein: 7

Hash Browns with Radish

Preparation Time: 20 minutes

Cooking Time: 15 minutes

Servings: 4

Ingredients:

- Shredded Parmesan cheese, 1/3 c.
- Garlic powder, ½ tsp.
- Salt
- Shredded radishes, 1 lb.
- Black pepper
- Onion powder, ½ tsp.
- Medium eggs, 4

Directions:

1. Set a large mixing bowl in a working surface.
2. Combine the seasonings, radishes, eggs, onion, and parmesan cheese
3. Arrange the mixture in a well-lined baking tray.
4. Set the oven for 10 minutes at 3750F. Allow to bake
5. Enjoy while still hot

Nutrition: Calories: 104, Fat: 6, Fiber: 8, Carbs: 5, Protein: 6

Baked Radishes

Preparation Time: 30 minutes

Cooking Time: 35 minutes

Servings: 4

Ingredients:

- Chopped chives, 1 tbsp.
- Sliced radishes, 15
- Salt
- Vegetable oil cooking spray
- Black pepper

Directions:

1. Line your baking sheet well then spray with the cooking spray
2. Set the sliced radishes on the baking tray then sprinkle with cooking oil
3. Add the seasonings then top with chives
4. Set the oven for 10 minutes at 375oF, allow to bake
5. Turn the radishes to bake for 10 minutes
6. Serve cold

Nutrition: Calories: 63, Fat: 8, Fiber: 3, Carbs: 6, Protein: 1

Coleslaw Avocado Salad

Preparation Time: 10 minutes

Cooking Time: 15 minutes

Servings: 4

Ingredients:

- White vinegar, 1 tbsp.
- Salt
- Olive oil, 2 tbsps.
- Black pepper
- Lemon stevia, ¼ tsp.
- Juice from 2 limes
- Mashed avocados, 2
- Chopped onion, ¼ c.
- Chopped cilantro, ¼ c.
- For coleslaw mix
- Salt, 1 tsp.
- Small red cabbage, ¼
- Shredded carrot, ½
- Lemon juice, ¼ c.
- Small green cabbage, ½
- Olive oil, ¼ c.
- Stevia, 1 tbsp.

- Zest of ½ lemon

Directions:

1. Set the mixing bowl in place to make the coleslaw salad
2. Add the mashed avocado and onions to coat well
3. Combine the seasonings, lime juice, vinegar, stevia, and oil in another bowl.
4. Add the mixture to the salad, mix to coat evenly
5. Enjoy

Nutrition: Calories: 481, Fat: 42, Fiber: 12, Carbs: 26, Protein: 6

Sherry watercress broth

Preparation Time: 20 minutes

Cooking Time: 15 minutes

Servings: 4

Ingredients:

- Sherry - ¼ cup
- Watercress- 6½ cups
- Chicken stock- 6 cups
- Coconut aminos- 2 tsp.
- Whisked egg whites of 3 eggs
- Shallots: chopped- 3
- Sesame seeds- 2 tsp.
- Salt and pepper

Directions:

1. Pour the stock into the pot and add sherry, coconut amino, salt and pepper and mix. Boil on medium heat.
2. Mix in watercress, shallots, and whisked whites and let boil.
3. Serve sprinkled with sesame seeds.

Nutrition: Calories- 73, carbs- 7, protein- 9, fiber- 2, fats- 7

Creamed cheddar Radishes

Preparation Time: 35 minutes

Cooking Time: 15 minutes

Servings: 1

Ingredients:

- Black pepper
- Halved radishes, 7 oz.
- Bacon slices, 2
- Chopped green onion, 1 tbsp.
- Sour cream, 2 tbsps.
- Cayenne pepper powder
- Salt
- Grated cheddar cheese, 1 tbsp.

Directions:

1. Set the radishes in a saucepan then add water.
2. Let it boil for 10 minutes over medium heat then drain the water
3. Set your pan over medium-high heat to cook the bacon to a crispy texture.
4. Drain the excess grease in a paper towel and reserve

5. Set the same pan again over medium heat then stir-fry the radishes for seven minutes

6. Stir in the seasonings, sour cream, and cayenne pepper powder for 7 minutes

7. Serve with crumbled bacon topped with cheddar cheese

Nutrition: Calories: 319, Fat: 25, Fiber: 3, Carbs: 8, Protein: 11

Mustard Egg and Avocado Salad

Preparation Time: 17 minutes

Cooking Time: 15 minutes

Servings: 4

Ingredients:

- Salt
- Mayonnaise, ¼ c.
- Medium eggs, 4
- Sliced avocado, 1
- Mustard, 2 tsps.
- Mixed lettuce leaves, 4 c.
- Chopped chives, 1 tbsp.
- Black pepper
- Minced garlic cloves, 2

Directions:

1. Set the cooking pan over medium-high heat.
2. Add water, eggs, and salt then allow to boil for about 7minutes.
3. Once boiled, drain the liquid, let cool then chop them.

4. Set a salad bowl in position to mix lettuce eggs and avocado

5. Toss with garlic, seasonings, and chives to coat

6. Combine the seasonings, mustard, and mayonnaise in another bowl

7. Add to the salad, toss and serve.

Nutrition: Calories: 278, Fat: 16, Fiber: 7, Carbs: 13, Protein: 12

Cucumber Avocado Salad mix

Preparation Time: 10 minutes

Cooking Time: 15 minutes

Servings: 4

Ingredients:

- Salt
- Sliced cucumber, 1
- Chopped avocados, 2
- Olive oil, 2 tbsps.
- Sliced onion, 1
- Chopped cilantro, ¼ c.
- Lemon juice, 2 tbsps.
- Black pepper
- Halved cherry tomatoes, 1 lb.

Directions:

1. Stir together cucumber, tomatoes, avocado, and onion in a salad bowl
2. Add the seasonings, lemon juice, and oil. Mix to coat well.
3. Serve cold topped with cilantro

Nutrition: Calories: 310, Fat: 27, Fiber: 1, Carbs: 16, Protein: 8

Fried Eggs with Kale and Bacon

Preparation Time 5 minutes

Cooking Time: 15 minutes

Servings: 2

Ingredients

- 4 slices of turkey bacon, chopped
- 1 bunch of kale, chopped
- 3 oz. butter, unsalted
- 2 eggs
- 2 tbsp. chopped walnuts
- Seasoning:
- 1/3 tsp salt

- 1/3 tsp ground black pepper

Directions:

1. Take a frying pan, place it over medium heat, add two-third of the butter in it, and let it melt, then add kale, switch heat to medium-high level and cook for 4 to 5 minutes until edges have turned golden brown.

2. When done, transfer kale to a plate, set aside until required, add bacon into the pan and cook for 4 minutes until crispy.

3. Return kale into the pan, add nuts, stir until mixed and cook for 2 minutes until thoroughly warmed.

4. Transfer kale into the bowl, add remaining butter into the pan, crack eggs into the pan and fry them for 2 to 3 minutes until cooked to the desired level.

5. Distribute kale between two plates, add fried eggs on the side, sprinkle with salt and black pepper, and then serve.

Nutrition: 525 Calories; 50 g Fats; 14.4 g Protein; 1.1 g Net Carb; 2.8 g Fiber;

Eggs with Greens

Preparation Time: 5 minutes

Cooking Time: 10 minutes

Servings: 2

Ingredients

- 3 tbsp. chopped parsley
- 3 tbsp. chopped cilantro
- ¼ tsp cayenne pepper
- 2 eggs
- 1 tbsp. butter, unsalted
- Seasoning:

- ¼ tsp salt
- 1/8 tsp ground black pepper

Directions:

1. Take a medium skillet pan, place it over medium-low heat, add butter and wait until it melts.

2. Then add parsley and cilantro, season with salt and black pepper, stir until mixed and cook for 1 minute.

3. Make two space in the pan, crack an egg into each space, and then sprinkle with cayenne pepper, cover the pan with the lid and cook for 2 to 3 minutes until egg yolks have set.

4. Serve.

Nutrition: 135 Calories; 11.1 g Fats; 7.2 g Protein; 0.2 g Net Carb; 0.5 g Fiber;

Spicy Chaffle with Jalapeno

Preparation Time: 5 minutes

Cooking Time: 10 minutes

Servings: 2

Ingredients

- 2 tsp coconut flour
- ½ tbsp. chopped jalapeno pepper
- 2 tsp cream cheese
- 1 egg
- 2 oz. shredded mozzarella cheese
- Seasoning:
- ¼ tsp salt

- 1/8 tsp ground black pepper

Directions:

1. Switch on a mini waffle maker and let it preheat for 5 minutes.

2. Meanwhile, take a medium bowl, place all the ingredients in it and then mix by using an immersion blender until smooth.

3. Ladle the batter evenly into the waffle maker, shut with lid, and let it cook for 3 to 4 minutes until firm and golden brown.

4. Serve.

Nutrition: 153 Calories; 10.7 g Fats; 11.1 g Protein; 1 g Net Carb; 1 g Fiber;

CONCLUSION

The things to watch out for when coming off keto are weight gain, bloating, more energy, and feeling hungry. The weight gain is nothing to freak out over; perhaps, you might not even gain any. It all depends on your diet, how your body processes carbs, and, of course, water weight. The length of your keto diet is a significant factor in how much weight you have lost, which is caused by the reduction of carbs. The bloating will occur because of the reintroduction of fibrous foods and your body getting used to digesting them again. The bloating van lasts for a few days to a few weeks. You will feel like you have more energy because carbs break down into glucose, which is the body's primary source of fuel. You may also notice better brain function and the ability to work out more.

Whether you have met your weight loss goals, your life changes, or you simply want to eat whatever you want again. You cannot just suddenly start consuming carbs again for it will shock your system. Have an idea of what you want to allow back into your consumption slowly. Be familiar with portion sizes and stick to that amount of carbs for the first few times you eat post-keto.

Start with non-processed carbs like whole grain, beans, and fruits. Start slow and see how your body responds before resolving to add carbs one meal at a time.

The ketogenic diet is the ultimate tool you can use to plan your future. Can you picture being more involved, more productive and efficient, and more relaxed and energetic? That future is possible for you, and it does not have to be a complicated process to achieve that vision. You can choose right now to be healthier and slimmer and more fulfilled tomorrow. It is possible with the ketogenic diet.

It does not just improve your physical health but your mental and emotional health as well. This diet improves your health holistically. Do not give up now as there will be quite a few days where you may think to yourself, "Why am I doing this?" and to answer that, simply focus on the goals you wish to achieve.

A good diet enriched with all the proper nutrients is our best shot of achieving an active metabolism and efficient lifestyle. A lot of people think that the Keto diet is simply for people who are interested in losing weight. You will find that it is quite the opposite. There are intense keto diets where only 5 percent of the diet comes from carbs, 20 percent is from protein, and 75 percent is from fat. But even a modified version of this which involves consciously choosing foods low in carbohydrate and high in healthy fats is good enough.

Thanks for reading this book. I hope it has provided you with enough insight to get you going. Don't put off getting started. The sooner you begin this diet, the sooner you'll start to notice an improvement in your health and well-being.